Silverton's Bobbie

His Amazing Journey — The True Story

To Liza —

Judith Kent

Silverton's Bobbie

His Amazing Journey — The True Story

by Judith Kent

Published by
Beautiful America Publishing Company
P.O. Box 244
Woodburn, OR 97071

Library of Congress Catalog Number 2004004332

0-89802-770-5

Printed in Korea

Dedication

To the 350 Urban Search and Rescue Teams of dogs and their partners who worked valiantly following the September 11, 2001 attacks on the World Trade Center, New York City.

Photo credit: Andrea Booher/FEMA photo

Table of Contents

Foreword

It was with keen interest that I read Judith Kent's manuscript, ***Silverton's Bobbie – His Amazing Journey – the True Story.*** The reasons were many. Local interest – a true story – a publishing candidate – but most importantly – it was about a Collie. The dog breed I love. My breed of choice.

However, the Collie in this true story goes back to 1923-24 – even before **my** time – and it is not about the beautiful, elegant show Collie of today, but about a working Scotch Collie, the type frequently referred to as a farm Collie.

As I read the story, I began to ask, "How in the world could this dog do this?" My experience with Collies has been in breeding, raising, training, showing and judging what I believe to be one of the most noble, proud breeds of all dogdom. Yet, in recent years, I have seen Collies consistently garnering high scores in obedience, agility, carting and herding – attesting to the fact that their regal beauty has not dulled the basic instincts that made them Collies in the first place.

I have purposely left out the one inherent instinct of the Collie in this story, as it deserves special attention. It is truly an inbred trait that over the years has been demonstrated time and again in the Collie breed. The homing instinct! That innate ability to travel over seemingly impassible territory – under the most adverse conditions – to reach its master, trainer, handler, or home!

We read of it in the books of Albert Payson Terhune and the unforgettable Eric Knight story, ***Lassie Come Home***. But these pale in comparison to the true story of Silverton's Bobbie. His story is so incredible – but how?

We need only look at history as our country fought our world wars. Conditions so heinous, our troops sought the assistance of Man's Best

Friend in the K-9 Corps. As dogs of all breeds were enlisted and trained for combat – facts about each breed became immediately known. The fierce fighters and attack dogs were the Doberman Pinchers and German Shepherds. Train as they might – they could not teach a Collie to attack on command. It was just not in their nature.

However, when important life and death decisions were too secret to trust to battlefield communications – it was the Collie that was called upon again and again to deliver the all-important message at night, through enemy lines, under constant fire, to headquarters often many miles away. And because of their basic homing instinct, they accomplished their missions repeatedly.

So it stands to reason, that this Collie, Bobbie, carrying that basic homing gene, was able to perform this seemingly impossible, absolutely amazing journey from Wolcott, Indiana, to Silverton, Oregon, over 2,000 miles, under the most adverse conditions in six months – on foot. Add to all these virtues mentioned above – those of love, devotion and faithfulness and you have Silverton's Bobbie – a true Collie story.

— ***Ted Paul***

Past President of The Collie Club of America, Inc.

Licensed AKC Collie Judge

Mark O. Hatfield served as governor of Oregon from 1959 to 1967 and as a U.S. Senator from 1967 to 1997. He is held in the highest regard having been honored in multiple ways over time for his leadership in bringing many fine things to Oregon.

His kind heart is evident, and his love for animals is appreciated. He first heard Bobbie's story when he was young. Perhaps this animal's strength of character, stout heart, faithfulness, loyalty, and affectionate nature inspired a young man named Mark, a long time ago...

MARK O. HATFIELD
OREGON

United States Senate

WASHINGTON, D.C.

Whenever I consider the values that a pet can help teach us, I recall a time years ago when my wife, Antoinette, and I were walking through the streets of a little community just before Christmas.

We came across a church that was displaying a living Nativity scene. People were dressed as Mary and Joseph; shepherds were there with their sheep, and there were cattle and a donkey. With this lovely group was a little boy and his dog, portraying a little shepherd boy.

We were impressed with this tranquil scene so much that we visited it every night, and we began to talk with the little boy. Never have I seen a boy who showed more love and kindness than this little fellow did to his dog. He was nine years old, and he told us he had owned his dog for his whole life.

On Christmas Eve, as we strolled past this scene for the last time, we saw the little boy sitting beside the manger crying. We stopped and gently asked him what was wrong. With tear-filled eyes he told us his dog had died--struck by a car which had skidded on the icy streets.

His grief was so great; yet he looked at us and said, "You know, I'll always miss my dog, but I will never forget our good times together--how I used to feed him and play with him. Even though I'm sad now, my parents said that I should be proud because my dog loved me because I was kind and always fed him and cleaned up after him."

As we walked away deep in our own thoughts, I knew how this young boy must have felt, but I also realized that his simple words bespoke a compassion, strength and love that would serve him well as he grew into manhood.

Yes, pets can be a precious gift. Treasure them and treat them with care and kindness. The compassion and responsibility you will gain in this effort will surely strengthen you as you grow into adulthood.

Mark O. Hatfield
United States Senator

Acknowledgments

These people provided advice, assistance and inspiration: Andrea Booher, Joan Dalton, V'Anne Didzun, Ross Eberman, Lois Feltus, Helen Frank, Gloria Garland, Rosemary Grover, Jack Hande, Senator Mark O. Hatfield, Tara Lubbers, Elise Moore/Federal Emergency Management Agency (FEMA), Oregon Historical Society, Oregon Humane Society, Sherwood Public Library, Silver Falls Library, Silverton Chamber of Commerce, Silverton Country Historical Society and Museum, The Appeal Tribune in Silverton, Kathy Steiner, Tigard Public Library, Vincent Till, and special thanks to my most helpful critic and strongest supporter, my husband, Bob.

A special thank you to:

- Vades Dickerson Crockett, the Brazier family member who was warm and helpful while sharing early Silverton history, letters, and photographs. Vades Crockett's grandfather was Frank Brazier, Bobbie's master. Vades is caretaker of Bobbie's memorabilia. With the Brazier family's permission, we are retelling Bobbie's story literally "in his master's voice."

- Dixie McCartney for her empowering suggestions and encouragement.

A $5.00 Puppy

Needing help with his farm animals, Mr. Frank Brazier, of Silverton, Oregon, purchased a puppy to raise as a herding dog. It was a six-week old bobtailed Scotch Collie. For the price of $5.00, he bought a dog destined to become not only a fine helpmate herding on his farm, but the most famous dog in the world at that time.

This warmhearted, humane master never spoke in anger, never ill-treated anybody or anything. Bobbie, like the Brazier's children, and Toodles – their frisky fox terrier, was never punished with more than a light scolding.

When Bobbie came to the farm, he soon became best friends with Toodles, who had come to Oregon with the Brazier family when they moved to Silverton in 1919. Toodles' faithfulness and intelligence made him a fine companion and role model for the new puppy.

The Collie became a fine, solemn, polite gentleman. He was valuable on the farm; he learned quickly to herd the family cow and horse to the barn daily. Clever with the sheep, he would drive them right and left, whichever way he was told, and never nipped a one.

He played with vigor and even laughed when he was a puppy. He would tease Snowbird until that cranky old goose would retreat to the barn. He aroused loud, threatening "Oink-oinks!" from a mother sow with many pink piglets. After he matured, he continued to herd the cow and horse to the barn and was always rewarded with praise from his master, "Well done, Bobbie."

During the days on the farm, several accidents left Bobbie with scars which later proved extremely helpful in silencing the skeptics who tried to cast doubt on the identity of Bobbie after the ordeal that was yet to come.

When Bobbie was about a year old, his terrier friend and playmate Toodles became ill and passed away. He was buried in back of their barn.

About that time, the Brazier family moved to downtown Silverton where they became proprietors of the Reo Café.

For Bobbie's own good, his master sold him to a friend who would be living on their farm. Bobbie was used to running free, and Mr. Brazier didn't feel he would be happy in the city. It was a great idea, but Bobbie wouldn't stay behind. He soon found the family in town and would walk into Silverton every Saturday, just to be with the Braziers, and he'd return to the farm on Monday mornings.

By August, 1923, it was evident that Bobbie would not adjust to a life away from his family. So, Mr. Brazier repurchased Bobbie, for three times the money, and he came to live with them.

In town, Bobbie had to put aside his farm games and behave himself. But, he was a well-mannered pet that was always at the entrance to his master's restaurant where he would greet, and be greeted by, the numerous patrons always coming and going. City folks, loggers, mill workers, and their children were daily visitors to the Reo.

That summer, Bobbie and some of his playmates shared many good times, such as tea parties at which he was a welcome guest and excursions with the neighbor boys down to the old swimming hole on Abiqua Creek. It was a great summer for Bobbie.

The Brazier homestead – Silverton.

"Climb in, Bob!"

Late that summer, the Braziers decided to take an automobile trip back East to visit friends and family. After much thought, they decided to take Bobbie with them. They left Silverton in their new Overland Red Bird automobile with their ecstatic dog riding on the running board or on top of the luggage.

Bobbie had a fine time during the trip. They allowed him freedom to run and explore when they stopped to eat or rest. Sometimes he would be gone for an hour or so, always to return, panting and grinning, as if trying to tell them all about his adventure, happy and refreshed.

Their first planned visit was in Wolcott, Indiana, having traveled 2,551 miles by odometer. They arrived on August 15, 1923.

SILVERTON

A Lost Pet

While Mrs. Brazier visited with their hosts, Mr. Brazier took Bobbie with him and drove to a local gas station to "fill 'er up." Mr. Brazier was inside the station when he heard Bobbie yelp. He rushed out to help, only to see Bobbie rounding a corner with a pack of wild, snarling dogs snapping at his heels.

Thinking Bobbie could take care of himself, his master drove back to the house, expecting Bobbie to be there waiting. Not so. Hour after hour went by, and they grew uneasy. They decided to drive slowly around town, honking and whistling. All to no avail. They finally gave up looking for Bobbie at midnight.

Trying her best to help, the town's sympathetic telephone operator called every local telephone in her directory seeking information about the missing pet. There was no word of a Collie having been seen anywhere.

The weekly newspaper went to press the next day, and Mr. Brazier asked the editor for his help. The editor loved Collie dogs, and was very willing. He published an advertisement that ran for three weeks, with no results. After weeks of searching, the Braziers sadly continued their trip as planned, and then headed home. All along the return route, they left word that if Bobbie showed up, he was to be shipped back to Silverton, at the Braziers' expense.

Bobbie ended up completely on his own that fateful day in Indiana. In a few seconds, he had become a stray, the loneliest word in the English language.

A Long, Lonesome Journey

A dog would not feel panic and fear as one of us would upon realizing our predicament – lost and always among strangers. Having never known abuse, he was not hesitant to approach people he met. It was reported that he readily jumped into cars waiting at intersections. Tail-wagging friendly, he would look into their faces, searching for someone familiar.

We now know some of the twists and turns he made before getting on course and traveling West consistently. Maybe it was magnetic pull from deep inside the earth that guided him through seven states over a six month period, all the way to the Willamette Valley and Silverton, Oregon.

Rivers to cross, endless open country to travel, mountains to climb. Time must have seemed dreadfully long to the desperate animal. Through autumn and winter months he was lost somewhere in the Middle Western states, climbing the Rocky Mountains in Colorado or Wyoming, tracking through Idaho's wilderness. A marvelous homing instinct was guiding him.

The weary miles of his quest led him over plains and prairies, by farms and through towns. It probably meant skirting lakes and fording streams and rivers, and as the weather worsened, crossing often on thick ice during that winter of 1924. People remembered seeing a starving-thin, resolute dog. At some farms, kind women reported having fed him. He would never stay long.

People back home in Silverton, having heard the word, hoped for the best. He had been born to smart, healthy parents, had always been well cared for by his master, and thus had the breeding and desire to make it. Good food, shelter, proper upbringing, and loving owners would all be things in his favor.

Willamette and Columbia Rivers freeze over – the winter of 1924.

The Birthday Wish

My favorite uncle always believed that he played a part in Bobbie coming home. As a youngster, his best friends had been invited and came December 19, 1923, to celebrate his ninth Birthday. After games and prizes, and Mother playing the piano while he was serenaded with the Birthday Song, she placed a beautifully decorated cake before him at the table. He says he squeezed his eyes shut and wished with all his might, then blew out all nine flickering candles with one breath.

Children often believe in miracles and enchantment. He had decided days before the party that he wanted to wish for something that, if it came true, would bring the most happiness to everyone – family and friends alike - "I wish Bobbie would come home safe and sound." However…

Months had gone by with no word. The Christmas holidays were not as joyful as usual because Bobbie was gone.

The winter of 1923-24 made his travels an almost constant struggle. With the onset of harsh weather, many wild animals he met would have been preparing for the cold days ahead. Some sought temporary shelter to survive the bone-chilling days and nights. Somehow, Bobbie's determination kept him moving westward, even during November through February. It was a winter that had to be endured!

Sometimes a miracle occurs only after several minor miracles of chance encounters and circumstances lay the groundwork. We can be thankful because we know that friendly people he met along the way allowed him to sleep on or under their porches or in their barns or kitchens when the thermometer plunged.

Maybe Mother Nature made it possible for other animals and birds to help him. Perhaps, in some fashion the animal world does look out for each other by communicating helpful encouragement, as minor as a "moo" or a "caw" or "hoot," may have led him to safe havens. Possibly, herons and ducks, circling and swooping low, they and chipmunks, rabbits, badgers and owls either chirping, or chattering and hooting were leading him along. Animals do communicate.

Back in Silverton, everyone became more aware of the weather while he was missing. If alive, they knew somewhere the dog was at its mercy. Uneasily, that fall the Braziers watched pairs of ducks and flocks of geese make their centuries-old flights south for the winter. Everyone knew of the fierce winds and bitter cold that was coming. The ground would harden. Snow would fall – softly fingering windows, blocking doors. How could Bobbie possibly be able to survive the winter of 1923-24?

Home, Sweet Home

Exactly six months after he was lost, on February 15, 1924, a miracle happened. Bobbie came home!

Nova, the Braziers' young daughter, was walking with a girlfriend in downtown Silverton near the Reo Café. Suddenly, Nova gasped and shocked her friend with, "Oh! Look! Isn't that Bobbie?"

Upon hearing her words, a thin, dirty and ragamuffin dog they saw just ahead of them turned, recognized Nova and fairly flew toward her – leaping up to cover her face with kisses while making half-strangled sobbing sounds of relief and delight.

It was Bobbie, without a doubt. The girls and he ran to the restaurant where the dog greeted Mrs. Brazier and Leona, Nova's older sister, with absolute joy. He rushed past curious, smiling bystanders and through the rooms searching for his master who having worked late the night before, was asleep upstairs.

Bobbie and Mrs. Brazier awakened him with their excitement. Nova called, "Wake up quick, Daddy, and see who's here!" Rubbing his eyes, Mr. Brazier thought he was dreaming as Bobbie licked his face while resting two dirty paws on his shoulders. The emaciated dog fell into his arms, whining and crying pitifully, seeming almost human in his joy at being home.

After resting, the famished dog devoured a choice meal of a thick, tender sirloin steak and a pint of cream. Then, as if he had never left, he sought his old bed in the basement, curled up, and for three days and nights he slept the sleep of absolute safety and complete exhaustion.

Bobbie slept and ate and when awake, would look imploringly at his family as if to say, "Please help me." His feet were tender and aching. Toenails worn down to the quick, his eyes inflamed, his coat matted and full of burrs. His next stop was a trip to the vet. A veterinarian examined him and said he had aged greatly during his six-month ordeal, but that his heart and lungs were still strong and healthy.

A few days later, when he was fully rested, Mr. Brazier took Bobbie out to visit their farm. It was evident he still remembered it. He inspected his old bed, and then suddenly seemed to recall something. The men watching got tears in their eyes when they saw him go to the spot where his childhood playmate, Toodles, was buried, digging as hard as he could, trying to get close to his old friend.

From his story thus far, you know of his personality, intelligence, and character. But his amazing journey would not have been possible without his ancestors' instincts, the treatment he received from a gentle and wise master, and the help of countless caring strangers along his way. A bit of warmth, a bite to eat, and kindness may well have saved the weary traveler's life.

He used his brain, as well as courage and wiry strength on that tremendous journey. He would pace himself, never too far at any one stretch so to become lame or enfeebled. He rested, accepted human kindnesses, and then kept going. However, on the very last leg of his journey, he let his keen longing to see his master again and his uncanny sense of being close make him careless of fatigue and hunger.

Mrs. Smith – Bobbie's Angel of Mercy

Portland, Oregon, almost became his sad last stop had it not been for a life-saving encounter.

The animal world must be thankful that there are people with affection and deep understanding in their minds and hearts. People that bring dignity and honor to the relationship between man and dog, or horse, or cat or any animal at all.

Of all the heartwarming accounts of kindnesses afforded Bobbie along his journey, I think the most poignant is that of Mrs. Mary Elizabeth Smith's compassionate care. She may well have saved his life during his last known stop before home. She met him on the last day of January in 1924. A demure little gray-haired widow, she lived alone in a modest home in east Portland, Oregon.

One day she was visiting in a neighbor's home and witnessed her wielding a broom to shoo away a gaunt, bedraggled, surely lost, dog from her door. Bobbie's serious condition was immediately apparent to Mrs. Smith when she first laid eyes on him.

The very next day, the same dog appeared at her door. Mrs. Smith loved animals and children, and when Bobbie's bewildered and deeply sad eyes met hers, like an angel of mercy, she knew she had to help him.

Weary, starving, bone thin, sorely limping, and with a matted coat, the dog appeared ready to drop. He appeared so weak that he could hardly stand.

She coaxed him into her kitchen and made a hasty bed for him by her warm cook stove. Offered water, he drank over a quart. Feeling safe, he relaxed while she spoke softly and lulled him to rest. He ate a bit of bread, too weak for more.

"Bide a wee," she crooned to the weary boy, remembering comforting words from her Irish grandmother. "Stay and rest a little while, lad." She said Bobbie turned sad, but thankful eyes to her face as he dropped his head in her lap, and with a little whimpering sigh, turned on his side with his injured paws before her.

She kept watch, like a mother over a sick child. While he slept, she bathed his sore feet with a comforting solution and dressed them with gentle, caring fingers.

He did not move for hours. He finally awoke when she spoke in soft tones and held a bowl of warm broth and bread near his muzzle. After taking a few laps, he relaxed and rested again.

A lonely widow, Mrs. Smith would have welcomed him to stay with her forever, but that was not to be. About five o'clock that evening, he revived. She opened the door for him to go out, thinking he would come back, but that was the last she saw of him – at that time.

Mrs. Smith and Bobbie were to meet again. A touching newspaper story was written by a reporter who saw him reunite with her weeks later when Bobbie was on exhibit for fans in Portland.

A small, elderly lady, she asked people in the admiring throng surrounding his protected area to please let her pass to get up close to Bobbie, "Her boy," as she called him. They obliged, and when Bobbie heard her sweet voice speaking softly to him and recognized the scent of her hands she placed on the fence, he pricked up his ears, whined and tried to lick the weathered hands that had cared for him. Tearful onlookers were touched to see him recognize her.

Her amazing grace and kindness was evident in the reporter's published story of their reunion that made her a celebrity, too.

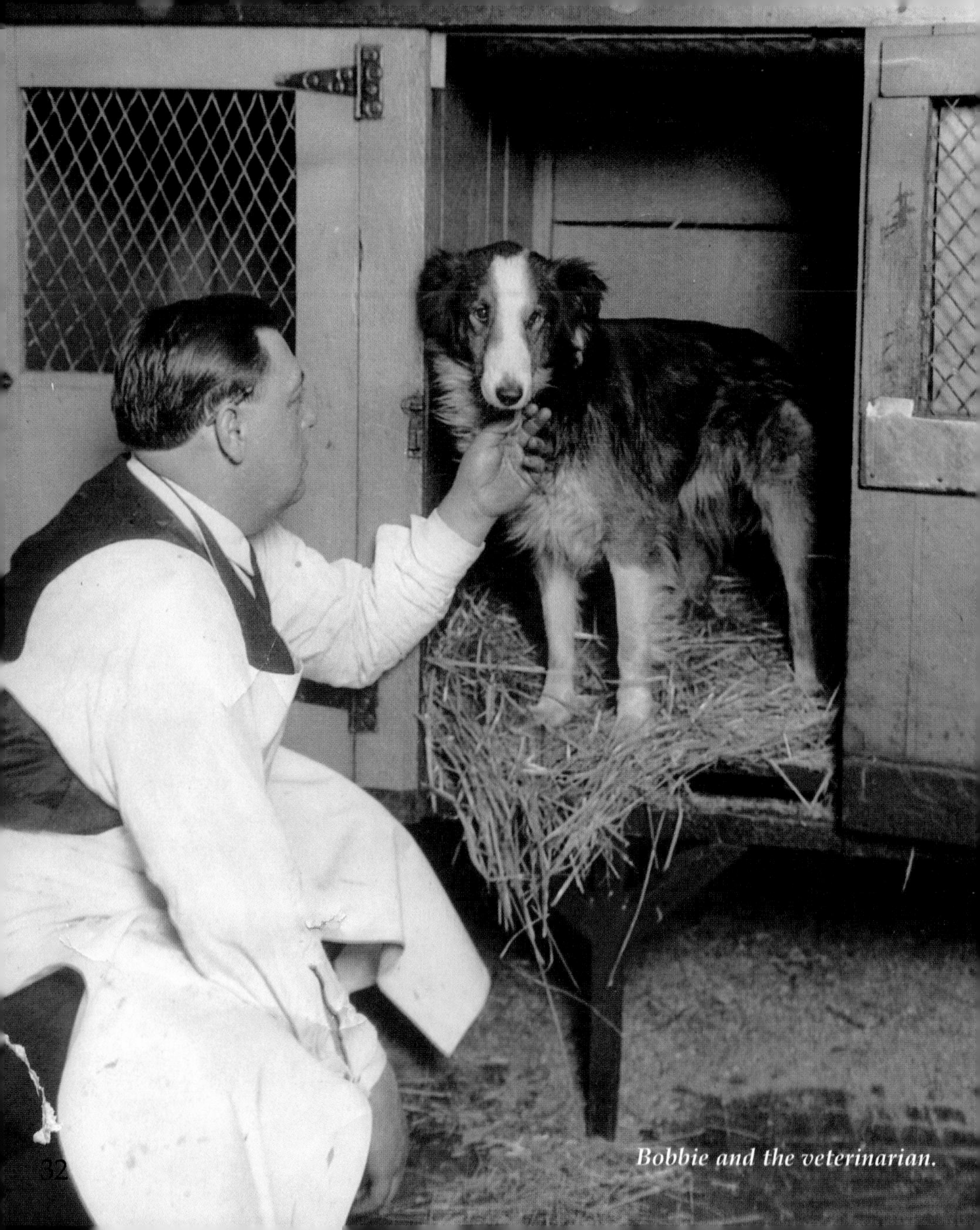

Bobbie and the veterinarian.

Other Good Samaritans He Met

Bobbie was three years old when he came home. Mature and deeply wise, he followed his "dog sense" and let his love for his family keep him going over 3,000 miles, counting detours reported by people who had housed and fed him on his way homeward.

Seeing him wounded and starving, some friend of dogs would feed and doctor him, and he would rest,. But as soon as he could, he would be up and away again. People reported he was always looking for someone and always in a hurry.

When he was home, news traveled like wildfire, by newspaper stories and by radio broadcasts, and Bobbie and Silverton became world famous overnight.

Letters poured in to his master that established his route. Bobbie, it seems, remained in Wolcott for several weeks searching for him. He then started for Oregon.

On the way east, Mr. Brazier housed his car every night in garages that we know as service stations today. The dog stopped at these establishments on his way west, and in some cases was fed and petted by the employees. It was a custom of the dog, letters said, to depart from the garages early in the morning without breakfast or water. Homeward bound, we now know.

The first sighting information to arrive in Mr. Brazier's mailbox was dated March 14, 1924. The truth of Bobbie's story is attested to by the many letters from people with whom he stopped for food and water and rest along the route, and by the fact that he got home. Never in a straight line, but almost always in the direction of his hometown.

Data was gathered all along the route from people who saw and fed Bobbie. *The Guinness Book of World Records* accepted the substantiating information and proudly included the Bobbie Story in their publication.

We know that strangers wrote of areas and campgrounds where he and his master and mistress had stayed that were revisited by the little traveler on his journey home. Folks reported having seen, fed and petted him after being touched by his gentle manner and hungry eyes.

Thanks to a handwritten letter to Mr. Brazier dated March 17, 1924, from Vinton, Iowa, we know that he stopped there:

> *"Dear Sir, - Sometime last fall, a dog answering to the name of Bobby stopped at our car and we took him in the house, but he would not eat a bite until he had looked all over the house, upstairs and down, and then he ate a good big meal and seemed quite contented all night. We gave him his breakfast in the morning and he stayed around just a little while and then left, and that was the last we saw of him. Did the horn of your car sound like a Dodge horn? We were stopped at the curb and just as we sounded the horn to attract someone's attention, the dog ran up and jumped right into the car as though it was his own. Our girls had owned a little dog named Bobby that had been run over and killed, and so they tried that name on this dog and would liked to have kept it here, but it just stayed the one night and then went on. It always seemed to be looking for someone. I just read in the* Cedar Rapids Gazette *of your dog traveling from Indiana to Oregon, and wondered if it could have possibly been the one that jumped into our car that night. Have you a Kodak picture of your Bobbie, if so, I would like to receive one just to see if it is the same dog.*
>
> *Respectfully,*
>
> *F. E. Patton*
>
> *P.S. Did you go East this way?"*

A very detailed letter arrived from Miss Ida Plum in Des Moines, Iowa, one of the first people to contact Mr. Brazier:

> *"My dear Mr. Brazier: I was greatly interested in an article appearing in the April number of* Moral Welfare *concerning the exploit of a Collie, "Bob," which you own. The picture so closely resembles a Collie we had the pleasure of entertaining during the fall of 1923 that I am prompted to write you in the hope of establishing his identity.*
>
> *The dog came to us wearing a heavy black strap collar. He made his appearance during the night; and finding my nephew sleeping on the porch, offered his paw to shake, after which he quietly went to sleep. In the morning after shaking hands with the family and receiving his breakfast, he departed in the direction of the tourist camp – which is only a few blocks from our home. In an hour or so he came back to us and took his abode. Although we were very fond of him, no effort was made to keep him. Almost every day he made the trip in the direction of the tourist camp, which led us to believe he had been lost from there. We tried different names, and found the name "Bob" seemed to suit him best. While with us, he disappeared for several days, and upon his return, we found that the heavy strap collar had been removed and a much lighter one substituted, to which a fragment of rope was attached, plainly showing that someone had tried to keep him. The latter part of November, 1923, - the day after Thanksgiving, to be exact – he again disappeared – and has never returned to us.*
>
> *It is unnecessary to say that we deeply regretted losing him, but have always hoped he found his way back to his own people. I am enclosing a couple of Kodaks showing the markings of the face."*

As a rule, Collies do not enjoy swimming, but we know that this gallant dog must have had to cross bodies of water that were obstacles. One poignant true story from Idaho was reported to a humane society by some homeless men, whose lives were touched by Bobbie. The hobos or tramps, as they were called, had set up camp by a rapidly flowing creek. One day, they were amazed to see a frightened dog hesitate on the creek bank across from them, then leap into the chilly water and swim across, struggling all the way. He emerged at their feet, water-soaked, cold, weak and bedraggled. Unselfishly, they shared their meager campfire-cooked meal with the famished animal.

Each man fondly remembered a pet he had loved when younger and enjoyed the stray's company during his short visit before he moved along on his journey. One man said their paths crossed months later in Salem, Oregon, and reported that Bobbie remembered him. In delight, the dog had greeted him with smiles and barks. The man suggested that he be named 'King of The Hobos,' but his master said that Bobbie wasn't exactly a tramp. He pointed his nose west, and kept going until he arrived home. He was not a vagabond.

One letter came from some folks who gave Bobbie a lift in their car to Denver, Colorado. While they went into a restaurant to eat, Bobbie jumped out of the car window and went back to his route. When the folks came back to their car, the dog was gone. Another car drove up, and they asked them if they had seen a dog. They replied, "Why, yes, we saw a Collie, and he was trotting along as if he knew where he was going."

Reported incidents like these reached Robert Ripley's desk. He was so moved that he created cartoons that spread Bobbie's fame worldwide. His "Believe It Or Not" daily pieces were read by readers of some 200 or more great daily newspapers in the United States as well as the great papers of foreign countries all over the world.

Literally millions of Earth's humanity were thrilled to read Bobbie's unusual story.

February 15, 1924: Bobbie Came Home!!!

A teacher in Silverton was so moved when she heard the good news that she sat down and composed a homecoming poem for Bobbie. She had the third and fourth grade students copy it from the blackboard as their penmanship drill for that day:

"Bobbie's Welcome"
Our Bobbie is home,
And we are so happy,
People are cheering,
And bands play on.

Hooray! Hooray!
Six months to the day,
Our wishes came true,
Wave the Red-White-and-Blue!

Later, she set it to music, and her class sang it to Bobbie and Mr. Brazier when they paid their school a visit after Bobbie was rested and feeling like himself again. She was proud when her class voted Bobbie "Citizen of the Week." She assigned the English lesson to be a "Welcome Home" letter to Bobbie. When all were finished putting their thoughts on paper, she read them to the class, and the students voted for the one that was to be mailed to the Brazier family on behalf of the class.

It was decorated beautifully and signed by all. This was the winning letter:

Dear Bobbie – WELCOME HOME!

We don't know how you did it, but we are all proud of you! When you are rested and well, our class would be honored to have you visit our school. Our principal will help us make it a special day for you, your master and all of the students and teachers.

We know your feet are sore, and that you are very tired. Please come just long enough for us to see you and give you a surprise present.

Your Friends,
Miss Goode's Class
Grades 3 – 4
Eugene Field School

Bobbie's Castle

Bobbie's Castle

When the public learned his remarkable story, Bobbie became a celebrity. That April 1924, he was invited to be the honored guest, prominently displayed at the Home Beautifying Exposition in Portland, sponsored by the Portland Realty Board.

A Portland home builder, J. W. McFadden, designed and built a modern miniature bungalow house for Bobbie that was displayed with the hero for all to enjoy that week. A policeman stood guard to protect the extraordinary exhibit. The house built for "The Wonder Dog" stands in good condition in the Pet Cemetery at the Oregon Humane Society in Portland.

The house weighed over nine hundred pounds and contained many of the comforts of a real home. Silk-curtained windows, even a fireplace.

After being displayed with his new house for the entire show, Bobbie was formally presented with a deed to the house in a special ceremony. After the show closed, Bobbie and his splendid house were transported by truck to Silverton, with many stops along the way for admiring fans to see the hero and his "castle."

They arrived in Silverton and were on display downtown before being delivered to the Brazier home. The very special building served as Bobbie's doghouse for the rest of his life.

Bobbie Is A Dad!!!

April 17, 1925, Bobbie became a father and set another record. A banner headline in many newspapers reported:

WONDER DOG BECOMES PROUD FATHER; Sixteen Pups and All of 'Em Boys

"I am daddy to 16 puppies this morning by my wife, Tippy. She is a Collie, too. All Bobbies,"

Bobbie the Wonder Dog

His best Collie characteristics were handed down to puppies such as the splendid Pal, Grand Marshall of the first Silverton Pet Parade that was held in 1932.

1927 - Time to Say Good-bye

In 1927, at only six years of age, Bobbie passed away. He had become ill, and the hardships he had endured had taken their toll. After his Homecoming in 1924, he lived a wonderful life with his family and friends, but all too short for those who loved and admired him.

In a solemn ceremony, he was laid to rest in the Pet Cemetery on the grounds of the Oregon Humane Society in Portland, Oregon. Over 200 people were there to pay their respects. A beautiful wooden casket was made especially for him. It was lined with green velvet.

A week later, the famous dog actor Rin Tin Tin, unable to be present at the ceremony, came from Hollywood, California, and laid a wreath on Bobbie's grave.

Silverton Pet Parade

A hometown pet parade was organized in 1932 and held to honor the memory of Bobbie, their self-reliant hero who had brought fame to the city. This was during the Great Depression and the parade organizers' goal was to bring inexpensive joy to the town's children. Merchants donated prizes which stimulated business for them during those hard times. The American Legion veterans were the first pet parade organizers and continued sponsoring the parade for many years thereafter.

The first parade was such a success for all of the town's animal-loving folks that the parade has been held during May every year since, always on the third Saturday. School bands accompany this parade that is the longest recorded annual Pet Parade in the United States.

Nowadays, young and old alike proudly walk, ride, push, or pull as they parade downtown with their pets. Animals and people of all ages are welcome. Cats, dogs, horses, bunnies, llamas, and a ladybug have all been crowd-pleasers. Clever costumes add to this colorful event. Trucks and even tractors move along with their happy participants. The Boy Scouts proudly lead the parade with Old Glory on display. Cameras are always clicking.

After the first Parade passed the judges, they were unanimous in awarding the Grand Prize for the best entry to Miss Vades Dickerson, 5, granddaughter of Bobbie's master.

Bobbie's son, Pal, was the Grand Marshall.

Epilogue

The City of Silverton
1854 – 2004
150 Years of Progress

Silverton natives can trace their beginnings back to the Oregon Trail pioneers. All feel great pride in this distinction and are proud to be Oregonians.

Only half of the 250,000 pioneers who traveled West on the Oregon Trail arrived at their destination. We are humbled by this fact. It resonates sadly even now, over 150 years later. As they followed the dream of reaching their Promised Land, energy, fortitude, labor and character kept them going. We can imagine the ache of homesickness many must have suffered. They endured illness, accidents, days without rain, swollen rivers, graves dug and passed. Many tears were shed. These humble people earned their honored place in American history.

And so it is with Bobbie, forever to be a heroic and valued figure in Silverton's colorful history and in the memories of all who knew this beloved pet and his story of infinite devotion.

In the year 2004, Silverton will celebrate its 150th year as an established city. In this time of nostalgia and commemoration, it seems fitting and proper to honor the four-footed individual who made the little city famous in 1924.

As I think about and wonder at Bobbie's story, I appreciate more and more what is good in life, what deserves honor and is worth preserving forever.

I know it opened my eyes to valuable lessons. Loyalty, love, perseverance, courage and kindness make all the difference. And, most of all, to the truth that character counts in all creatures, great and small.

Bobbie was dogdom's Lewis and Clark rolled into one. We can hardly imagine how he, alone, managed to find his way over thousands of miles with nothing but himself and his homing instinct leading him home. He, too, deserves our respect.

When his story became known, many honors and gifts were bestowed upon the humble pet. Besides dozens of letters and honors, he received a gold collar, so many medals that they could not all be mounted on his harness, gifts from all over Europe and even from Australia. The keys to the Canadian city of Vancouver, B.C., arrived.

A fence had to be built through which Bobbie could be admired, but not touched. Constant petting by his thousands of admirers had made his body tender and sore.

After his ordeal, his beloved family cared for him more dearly than ever, and felt the greatest of pride in their gentle Collie – The Wonder Dog of Oregon.

Silverton's Bobbie the Wonder Dog made history. *The Guinness Book of World Records* later published his remarkable accomplishment in these words:

> *In 1923 a Collie dog named "Bobbie," lost by his owners while they were on holiday in Wolcott, Indiana, turned up at the family home in Silverton, Oregon, 6 months later, after covering a distance of over 2,000 miles (3200km). The dog, later identified by householders who had looked after him along the route, had apparently traveled back through the states of Illinois, Iowa, Nebraska and Colorado, before crossing the Rocky Mountains in the depth of winter and then continuing through Wyoming and Idaho.*

Frank Brazier wrote and thus preserved a detailed description of his experiences with his Bobbie for us to marvel at so many years after the event. We have merely gathered his notes – viewed the countless eyewitness reports, the newspaper accounts, and all the other authenticating documents – to put this story together. Facts you read here are true, and they weave an unforgettable tale.

The End

Illustrations by
Eugene Nelson